The Little Ache

The Little Ache
– a German notebook

Ian Wedde

Victoria University of Wellington Press

Victoria University of Wellington Press
PO Box 600, Wellington
New Zealand
vup.wgtn.ac.nz

A catalogue record is available from the
National Library of New Zealand.

ISBN 9781776564262

Published with the support of a grant from

Printed by Blue Star, Wellington

These poems began and in many respects ended as diary notes made while in Berlin and the north of Germany around Kiel in 2013–14, when I had the good fortune to be awarded the Creative New Zealand Berlin Writer's Residency. In the time margins around the residency's main commitment, I stalked the family ghosts of German ancestors and obscure relatives and associates, in particular those connected to my great-grandmother Maria Josephine Catharina née Reepen, whose family lived in the north, close to the Danish border near Kiel. Among many surprises I found a relative of hers called Klaus Groth (1819–99) – 'the founder of Plattdüütsch dialect literature' – and a friend of Johannes Brahms; Brahms made some of Groth's mawkish poems into songs that were sung by Maria's sister Sophie. There's a statue of Groth in Kiel. I wasn't able to discover what became of Sophie nor why my great-grandmother embarked for New Zealand by herself in 1875 and married a runaway sailor, Heinrich August Wedde. No one knows why Great-Grandfather Heinrich had to make himself scarce from Germany, but in the Staatsbibliothek in Berlin I found a firebrand *Sozialdemokrat* poet relative-of-some-kind called Friedrich Christoph Johannes Wedde, who died in 1890 at the age of forty-seven after publishing a mostly unread panegyric to the Paris Commune martyrs of 1871 and corresponding with Friedrich Engels in London. Perhaps my fugitive great-grandfather Wedde was also a radical Marxist, though what I know of his New Zealand history makes this implausible. These and other ghosts whispered to me as I enjoyed daily life in Berlin, including the chance to eavesdrop on a conversation between Frau Angela Merkel and the singers Wolf and Pamela Biermann in the bar at the Berliner Ensemble. At other times I bought buckwheat honey, a floor mop, and a bike for Donna, drank morning coffee at Café Cortado, and had my German mocked by a pedantic librarian in the Staatsbibliothek on Potsdamerstraße as I tried to borrow Johannes Wedde's book.

1

Vergiss deine Tasche nicht
'Don't forget your bag'
my great-grandfather Heinrich August Wedde's
ghostly admonition
at customs clearance

but I did
distracted by what might have been
the irritable clatter in the galley
where my ancestor was heating soup
as the *Robin Hood* leaned across an ebb tide
out of some harbour in Poitou-Charentes
whose meandering deltas may have reminded him
of the waterways of his first debouch
out of Kiel or Hamburg
a kid with horizons in his eyes
with Goethe in his kit
but no idea where he'd be lugging the *Faust*
my father heard him shouting
from the bed he took to on pension night
with a skin-full of schnapps
at York Terrace, Blenheim.

The same bed where pneumonia
silenced his *Modersprak*
after he was pushed into the river
(some say)
where he was peacefully fishing
in 1915
(because he was German).

How thick is the space
between what Heinrich had in his bag
and what he left behind
or just forgot as it may be
about the time he jumped ship
from the *Lammershagen*
in Wellington Harbour in 1875
making himself scarce up-country
until such time as he came back
after a prudent year
with his bag and its frugal contents
to marry my great-grandmother
Maria Josephine Catharina Reepen
of the straight back and forthright gaze?

I recover my bag
from an amused customs official
at Berlin's Tegel Airport
and make my way into the city
which seems both foreign and not
perhaps like Heinrich August
caring little about the difference between what I carry
and what I don't.

In the courtyard outside my new home
a chestnut tree drops wads of wet brown leaves
and I'm only a little tempted by the folly
of wondering if it forgets them
for the fresh ones it will grow in spring.

2

Im Hochsommer besuchen die Bienen viele unterschiedliche Blüten
'In high summer the bees seek many different flowers'
caught my eye on the jar of honey
in the organic shop around the corner
in Boxhagenerstraße
but outside it was already getting dark
at 4:30 in the afternoon
and the warm bars were filling
with a buzz of patrons
dipping their lips
into fragrant brews
jostling each other in a kind of dance
I didn't join
(I didn't know how to
couldn't 'find my feet')
but took home my jar of Buckweizenaroma
buckwheat/bookwise aroma
and sampled some on a slice
of Sonnenblumenbrot.

3

'. . . rocks on the one hand and dreams on the other –
they are things of this world.'
(Clifford Geertz) –

I wake up from a dream about my father
Frederick Albert Wedde
whose name was both a dream
my great-grandfather brought ashore in his bag
and the thing I touched
when I said goodbye to the stone-cold body
of Heinrich's grandson
that was no longer my father
who'd become a kind of inscription:

> Heinrich August and Maria Josephine Catharina
> their children
> Reinhold Henry
> William Frederick
> Elisabeth Frederika
> Bertha Mary
> Albert Augustus (my grandfather)
> Frederick Alexander
> Herman Conrad
> Herbert Edward.

4

. . . dichte und schöne Fenster.

'Well-sealed and nice windows' are what Frau Merkel
the German Chancellor
thinks epitomise what's best
about her country
its core value
the key performance indicator
establishing its point of difference
from draughtier places
or places where the cold gets in
as perhaps it did up north along the Baltic shoreline
when Heinrich and Maria were young
bashing the pump to get ice out of its spout
(I imagine)
while a warm breeze from the Pacific
pressed its dream to their chilblained cheeks
with an aroma of tropical coconuts
whenever the bread oven was opened.

It's four in the afternoon
and already a three-quarter moon
floats white-faced like a seasick sailor
in the darkening sky
above the apartments across the street
where well-sealed windows
are lit from within like little dioramas
whose fragments of life
flit across the provisional warmth of the present.

5

Min Modersprak, wa klingst du schön!
'My mothertongue, how sweet you sound'
wrote Klaus Groth
(1819–99)
the founder of Plattdüütsch dialect literature
so I'm told
by the lowlands-1.net website
where my distant relative appears in a portrait
with wavy silver hair
which I imagine will be repeated
by the statue of him I've heard about
somewhere in Kiel
up there on the freezing Baltic coast
where his head's been crowned with snow
in the hometown of his cousin
my great-grandmother
Maria Josephine Catharina
which I hope to visit when the weather warms up
and the distinguished locks of Klaus Groth
will have thawed to the auburn tint of bronze
as if henna'ed in defiance of time.

I arrived with little enough German in my kit
let alone the sort Klaus loved
as if language was a mother
at whose breast he'd drunk speech
which his friend Brahms made into songs
sung by Maria's sister Sophie
who 'cut some ice' as a soprano
in the operatic world up there.

How much English
did Maria come ashore with
in 1876
and was it the Brahms settings of Groth's *Modersprak*
that she sang while taking loaves from the oven
in the draughty kitchen
in Bute Street, Wellington
while an icy southerly rattled the windows
weder dicht noch schön?

6

Von allem Leid, das diesen Bau erfüllt,
Ist unter Mauerwerk und Eisengittern
Ein hauchlebendig, ein geheimes Zittern.
'From all the suffering that fills this building
there is under masonry and iron bars
a breath of life a secret tremor.'

In the Moabit Prison Memorial
where Albrecht Haushofer's words
incised in the back wall
already wear the weary patinas of time and weather
or more probably the perfunctory smears
of graffiti cleansing
I'm assailed by a nipping dog
whose owners apologise in terms I don't quite understand
though the dog does
and retreats ahead of the half-hearted kick
I lack the words to say isn't called for.

The horizon's filled with gaunt cranes
resting from the work of tearing down or building up
the forgettable materiality of history
an exercise one might say
in removing that which was draughty
and replacing it with that which can be sealed.

Or as it may be
tearing down the sealed panopticon
but making space to train dogs in.

7

Ineradicable
I wake up with this word in my head
out of a dream
that's already been eradicated
but by what agency
and did it even exist
and if it did exist
and has been eradicated
then why was it important
to leave the word *ineradicable* behind?

As a kind of taunt perhaps
to that which has been uprooted
Heinrich and Maria
but replanted in the thick space
between words and genes
and in me
somewhere
like a dream.

8

Eine kleine Enkelin
A little granddaughter
Cara Lilly Malane
born 23 November 2013
along with a new word
Enkelin.

So
there.

9

Ach, die erste Liebe
macht das Herz mächtig schwach
Und die zweite Liebe
weint der ersten nur nach
Doch die dritte Liebe
schnell den Koffer gepackt
schnell den Mantel gesackt
und das Herz splitternackt

Ah, that first love
greatly weakens the heart
And the second love
cries only after the first
But the third love
quickly packs the bag
quickly bags the coat
and the stark naked heart

Ach der erste Krieg
da ist keiner schuld
Und der zweite Krieg
da hat einer Schuld
Doch der dritte Krieg
ist schon meine Schuld
ist ja meine Schuld
meine Mordsgeduld

Ah, with the first war
no one's to blame
And so the second war
has a debt there
But the third war

is already my fault
   is my fault
      my murder of patience

Ach, der erste Verrat
   kann aus Schwäche geschehn
Und der zweite Verrat
   will schon Orden sehn
Doch beim dritten Verrat
   must du morden gehn
     selber morden gehn
      und das ist gescheh'n

Oh, the first betrayal
   can happen out of weakness
And the second betrayal
   wants to appear religious
But with the third betrayal
   you have to commit murder
     go and kill yourself
      and that is what happens.

Thus the famous song by the Georgian poet Bulat Okudzhava
sung at the Berliner Ensemble
on 12 December 2013
by Wolf and Pamela Biermann.

'This huge little poem
illuminates the whole world –
between the poles of the private and the political,'
announced Biermann (in German).

Afterwards
Wolf and his wife Pamela
sat drinking in the theatre cantina with Frau Angela Merkel
(she of the *dichte und schöne Fenster*)
and they discussed what to do
about Vladimir Putin
while I tried to overhear and translate
at the next table.

This is a true story
whose moral escapes me
as does an adequate translation
of Okudzhava's wonderful song
which the conversation at the chancellor's table
seemed prosaically to resemble.

10

Fünf Narren jeden Tag
'Five fools every day'
said the smiling customs official
when I went to pick up the bag I'd forgotten
along with most of the German
I was taught by Robert Lübker
in 1956 when my brain was young
and I learned without trying
but fifty-eight years later
I remembered enough to reply
Und jetzt der sechste
and now the sixth
surprising myself
as I wheeled my bag out the door.

The last time I saw Robert
was in 1995 in Hamburg
he was ninety years old
and wept politely into the handkerchief he'd prepared
for that purpose
as we said goodbye at the station.

He waved the same handkerchief
as the train pulled out
which was typical of Professor Lübker's
philological precision
as if his handkerchief were language
capable of various careful deployments.

Likewise his discourse over lunch
(fresh asparagus and a glass of Riesling)
which was of Johann Gottlieb Fichte

and his belief in the social nature of self-knowledge
which my old teacher explained to me
in between vigorously chewing
the way I remember him chewing words
for example *Und jetzt der sechste*
(little bit of spit).

I'm told
that my great-uncle Rheinhold
known as Ren or Dick
born in 1877 in Bute Street, Wellington
the oldest of my grandfather's siblings
lived out his days in Auckland
in the house of my second cousin Peter
arriving from the King Country with a cabin trunk
which he had not forgotten to fill
with the complete works of Fichte
and needless to say therefore
of Kant also
whose difficult style
and dense language
Johann Gottlieb was sometimes accused of mimicking.

In whose bag did those books come ashore
and where are they now
and by whom were they forgotten
and what did my great-grandmother Maria Reepen
choose to forget
and Heinrich August
what did he leave behind
on a day when someone waved a handkerchief
from the wharf at Kiel or Hamburg
as *jetzt der nächste Narr*

shipped out looking for the horizon
beyond which he might come to know himself
among different people?

11

Regentropfen aus den Bäumen
'Raindrops from the trees'
was inscribed by Klaus Groth on the 2nd of May 1856
in a copy of the third edition of his book of poems *Quickborn*
to which had been added the High German
Hundert Blätter: Paralipomena zum Quickborn
('One Hundred Leaves: Supplement to Quickborn')
for his new friend Johannes Brahms
to whom he was connected
through the family of his wife Doris
who was modest about her musical accomplishments
but unstinting in admiration
for her husband's poetry.

Brahms set 'Regentropfen' to music in 1871 (Op. 59, 4)
but didn't publish it in his lifetime.

Groth's 'hundred leaves' grew not from the *Modersprak*
for which he became famous
after the publication of *Quickborn* in 1852
but from the High German of *Hundert Blätter*
for which he was mocked
and soon forgotten.

The *Plattdüütsch* dialect of the composer's childhood in
          Hamburg
'is something different from language'
Brahms demurred.

'I've tried it
it doesn't work.'

But perhaps he anticipated the titters
of his sophisticated Viennese audience
rather than the grateful fervour of his home-town.

Even his one attempt
Da geit en Bek de Wisch entlang
was first set to music in 1862
by the eighteen-year-old upstart Friedrich Nietzsche.

The Brahms setting descended into obscurity
first published in 1889 or 99
and performed for Groth's eightieth birthday in 1899
and then
'lost'.

Brahms already dead two years earlier
having earlier still
wounded the poet by declaring
'You know nothing about music.'

The forgiving
and helpful letters of Klaus Groth
as well as the helpful
and affectionate letters of his wife Doris
which Brahms seldom answered.

In September 1878
at a rehearsal of works by Brahms in Hamburg
the Danish composer Niels Gade saw Groth
'a ridiculous figure
a long thin person who was sitting silently by himself
and was in peculiar-looking clothes.'

'. . . a sincere quiet man.'

Perhaps unable to know himself
among his own people
but I want to add
as a young schoolteacher in Heide
rumoured to have tossed poems
through the open bedroom window
of 'dark-haired, brown-eyed'
Mathilde Ottens.

12

Stricher
was what I
a stranger to the German language
went asking for
in the street that's my home for now
and was directed
with a funny look
to the nearby junction with Revalerstraße
where the Black dope-dealers hang out
which didn't seem right
since what I wanted as presents
for a friend's little daughters
were the knitting devices
with which kids make tubes of coloured wool.

Seems I'd been inquiring
where I could find a rent-boy.

Strickeliese
was what I should have been asking for
explained my amused neighbour in the flower shop
adding straightforwardly
that the *'liese'* part of the word
was there because the woollen tubes
manufactured by the *Strickeliese*
resemble 'a woman's you-know'.

13

ende/anfang
ende/anfang
ende/anfang
On the programme board
of the anti-capitalist agitprop
Theaterkapelle at 99 Boxhagenerstraße
next to the old graveyard
where young women wheel prams
so their babies can hear the birds
making an impatient racket in the bare trees
an abrupt announcement appeared
in mid-winter
a single word
lowercase
repeated three times
in a column
ende
ende
ende
(it's over)
but beside each word
a neighbourhood tagger had written
anfang
anfang
anfang
(start again).

The embourgeoisement of the neighbourhood
proceeds apace
and the Theaterkapelle is one of its casualties
as predicted in its last production
Die Kunden werden unruhig

The audience is getting restless
to which the Freitag salon blogger Peter Nowak had added
und vielleicht auch wütend
and perhaps angry as well.

As the rents go up
and façades are scrubbed
dichte und schöne Fenster installed
GDR-vintage furniture
overpriced in the Sunday fleamarket
I find myself wondering
what kind of fresh start
I have the right to hope for
having come only this far
having barely tested my restlessness
let alone my anger.

And what kind of restlessness
let alone anger
drove my great-grandmother
Maria Josephine Catharina Reepen
to declare *Anfang*
beside a disreputable runaway sailor's name
Heinrich August Wedde
at the end of the earth?

14

Viel Glück und Freude!
'Good luck and happiness!'

I got lucky twice
when Donna came into my life
about thirty years ago
because Mischa came with her.

I remember his spaghetti legs around my neck
when I carried him on my shoulders
for a protest march along Lambton Quay.

What were we protesting about?
Not good fortune in my case
because just then I had plenty of it.

He was yelling
'One two three four
we don't want your racing score!'
– maybe he didn't like the odds.

But the odds were good
Fortune was marching with us
and because Mischa was in my life
(along with Donna)
about five years ago
Laura was too! And because Laura was
so was Bella and, before long, Cara!

Not such a bad score.
How lucky can you get?
But this isn't about me.

I'm writing this in Berlin in winter
after walking in Treptower Park
in the snow among bare trees
next to the frozen river Spree
which is a long way from my good fortune
back there in Auckland in summer
where the pōhutukawa will be shedding crimson flowers
into the flowing tide
at the bottom of Hamilton Road.

You can see the warm water moving there
because the crimson surface is moving
but the pale unmoving ice
on the surface of the river Spree
tells me that even if you can't see fortune's flow
it's still there
under the hard stare of the present moment
and it's moving us all together
in the same direction
towards the next moment
when we'll raise our glasses
to the luckiest of us all
Mischa, Laura, Bella and Cara
on their wedding day.

'Good luck!'

My words shoot out as misty breath
above the mug of hot Glühwein mit Rhum
I'm sipping in Treptower Park
and the startled strangers standing nearby
all lift their drinks as well
and we all shout together

Viel Glück und Freude!

Good fortune and happiness
to Mischa, Laura, Bella and Cara!

(Noch einmal!
Viel Glück und Freude!)

15

... man is an animal suspended in webs of significance
he himself has spun.
(Clifford Geertz) –

The ice has melted on the Spree
people walk beside it
with their hats off
as if seeking a different warmth
than the humid recirculation
of mind-heat.

That sunlight on the water though
might almost resemble ice
and the flotillas of waterfowl
with dabs of white
atop their beaks
might be thought of
as the icebreakers of spring.

This seems to be approaching a conclusion
but what that might be
I've no idea.

Unless it's to do
with those 'webs of significance'
dear Professor Geertz
believes we spin.

In this instance
out of very little.

16

Dies ist nun alles und ist nicht genug.
'This is all there is and it's not enough'
is the line by Bertolt Brecht
that I find myself thinking about
at ten in the morning
when the sun doesn't quite rise above
the apartment buildings
in Simon-Dachstraße
where I'm drinking a coffee
outside the café Cortado.

But spring is in the air
the café's outside tables
all sport a single unopened crocus in a little vase
and though I know about the situation
Brecht was addressing
in my mind I'm already measuring how long it will be
before the sun gets above the apartments
and I head north to the summer Baltic
to look for traces
of the ancestral dissatisfactions
to which I owe my existence.

17

Wo nur ein Blümchen blühte,
Das blühten gleich sie mit
'Wherever a simple flower bloomed
They* bloomed as well'
*(Klaus Groth's childhood dreams)
but the present in which he imagined them
(the dreams)
was maudlin to say the least
and I want to admonish my late sentimental cousin
with advice to live in the present
and not yearn for what's gone
especially your infancy
but of course it's too late now.

Wie traulich war das Fleckchen
'How cosy was that little spot'*
*(Klaus's bassinet)
published by Brahms in 1874
as 'Heimweh I' Op. 63, 7
for which the setting is enchanting
while the lyric
reveals Brahms to have had as wet an ear for language
as Klaus's was mawkish.

Purple yellow and white crocuses
have appeared in clusters
under the bare trees in Treptower Park
and moles have snouted their long sleeps
up into the sunlight
in the form of earth mounds.

I eat a bowl of bad pea soup
at the Stern und Kreis Hafengarten
next to a man who looks like W.H. Auden
who drains his wine glass with a deep sigh
and points the cigarette in his mouth
towards the sun.

Plume of vapour
from the power plant's smokestack
jet-trails across the blue sky.

I catch the S-Bahn back to Frankfurter Allee
and at 4:23 in the afternoon
a bee flies past my third-floor window.

Everything that was thick and complex
is becoming thin and familiar
or else everything that had become familiar
thickens in the present moment.

18

Aber es kostet viel
worries the friendly woman
in Jana's Haushaltswaren in Frankfurter Allee
when I push my Sprintus Magic Click floor mop
across the counter
but I don't care
because none of the cheap ones
has lasted more than a week
and my floor is covered by the dust of spring
the rooms inhale through windows wide open
for the first time in months.

I inhale this chest-clogging *Staub* also
and add the word to my vocabulary
of household hygiene
along with *Schmutz* and *Kalk*
the grime and lime of here-ness
and cousin Klaus's memory-freshening *Blümchen.*

19

Bildung
is the word that springs to mind
as I watch from my window
the courtyard birds
building their nests in spring
the long-tailed Elster magpie-crows
credited with self-awareness
and huge brains
by Helmut Prior at Goethe University in Frankfurt
restoring the shambolic penthouse
at the top of the chestnut tree
which will soon shelter their young
with its fresh growth of leaves.

If Bildung is the story of individuation
with which Goethe's hapless Werther
franchised the metaphysics
of wishy-washy Romantics
but if as Hegel believed
being-at-home-with-yourself is accomplished
through the advancement together
of personal growth and social relationship
through a rigorous building from negations
(such as unrequited love)
and Fichte through the social nature of self-knowledge
and Geertz through webs of significance
(read nests)
then the prankish Elster are highly evolved
getting on with here-ness
being at home
exchanging raucous jokes
flirting a little bit

making room for the stupid pigeons
and the randy sparrows
and not too disheartened when they drop their nest-sticks
on the heads of the humans below
who could learn something
as I hope I do from watching them
while prolonging my morning coffee
and thinking I should get out more.

20

Die Leiden des jungen Werthers.
Meanwhile the pigeon I've named Werther
fastidiously pokes feathers
into an improbable nest
at the ill-chosen extremity of a branch
hoping to win the love of his Lotte
and then just as fastidiously
plucks them out again
and drops them on the cat
basking in the bicycle park.

From my kitchen window
I see the cat's mouth
open up at the tree
in what is at once a snarl and a yawn.

Bildung through negation
Hegel's self-improvement dialectic
or in this case not giving a fuck.

21

Oberbaumbrücke
is one of those contrapuntal German nouns
that should be simple but isn't
unless you think
'upper-tree-bridge' is simple.

The long trailing tresses of the willows
have turned pale green
and are thrashing in the wind
on the Kreuzberg side
of die Oberbaumbrücke
over the storm-churned Spree.

They are the uneasy ghosts of spring.

Gritty gusts
blow rubbish along the embankment.

In a crappy nook
a graffitied child clenches a raised fist.

Yesterday at the Leipzig Book Fair
I listened to a fierce debate
about the situation in Ukraine
and later visited the Nikolaikirche
where Johann Sebastian Bach had played the organ.

One situation was loud with discord
the other's efflatus a ghostly counterpoint.

On the train back to Berlin
I received a text from Donna
who'd been rocking our granddaughter Cara to sleep.

My bag from the Book Fair
had a paradoxical misquote from Ezra Pound on it:
Literatur ist Neues,
                    das neu bleibt.

The train was speeding at 200 kilometres an hour
towards the place I'm calling home
because it's haunted by ancestors who left slowly
but surely
thereby established the first term
of my contrapuntal neologism:
Endeanfang.

22

Bestellen am Tresen
'Order at the counter'
of Café Cortado
whose recalcitrant crocuses of a week ago
have opened in morning sunlight
where the sun that rises above the apartment buildings
across the street
now warms their tabletop vases
as if *am Tresen bestellt*
von meinem sprachneuschöpfungen Freund
'*Endeanfang*' –
as if ordered at the counter
by my neologistical friend
'Endstart'.

23

Der kleine Mann mit dem interessanten, ausdrucksvollen Kopfe
auf einem leider verwachsenen Körper
war ein glühender Sozialdemokrat;
konnte aber erst später öffentlich als solcher auftreten.

Why do we say
'the ghost of a smile'
and why did I ask myself that
when what I saw was
'the smile of a ghost'
on the 'interesting, expressive' face
of the little firebrand with the sharp blue eyes
who was talking with fluent zeal
in the Association of Left Publishers precinct
at the Leipzig Book Fair?

The 'little man with the interesting, expressive head
on an unfortunately deformed body'
could have been the ghost
of the *Sozialdemokrat* described by Wilhelm Joseph Blos
(1849–1927)
in his *Denkwürdigkeiten eines Sozialdemokraten*
(*Memorabilia of a Social Democrat*)
first published in 1914
when Blos was already sixty-five
and lived to be seventy-eight
whereas the little withered man
my distant relative
Friedrich Christoph Johannes Wedde
died in 1890 at the age of forty-seven.

24
In
seine mit Geist und Humor gewürzte Konversation
I recognise the 'alert and humour spiced conversation'
of my living cousins
as if our remote *Vetter*
still refused to shut up.

25

However in
seine oft sehr hübschen Verse
konnten wegen des gelehrten Ballastes,
mit dem sie gepackt waren, nicht in die Masse dringen
it's the ghost of a smile I see
when I read what Joseph Blos thought
of Johannes Wedde's poems
which though 'often very beautiful
didn't sink in with the wider public
on account of the scholarly ballast
with which they were packed'.

26
The vanity of art
(Milan Kundera) –

In spring
I return to the Moabit Prison Memorial
Haushofer's words are still there
writ large on the back wall
they seem a little faded
but that could be the effect
of lucid sunshine
which elongates the speeding shadows
of dogs chasing Frisbees
and picks out
the filigreed patterns of trees
beginning to be crowned
with pale baldachins of leaves.

The girl panhandling on the footpath
at Warschauerstraße Station
has scrawled an unambiguous request
on the cardboard placard
her dog's sleeping head
seems to be dreaming:
'cash for beer and weed
and food for the dog'.

What the ghosts of Moabit are saying
I find harder to understand.

The memorial park's stark absences
move me

and the minimal architectural features
seem respectful and not vaunting.

But the silence here
which the happy dogs
vociferous nesting birds
industriously rebuilding cranes
and agitated railway station
do not fill

that silence

crowds into a place in the mind
that scepticism can't reach
where ghosts gather obliviously
without caring if I sense them
or if any of this exists.

27

Patriotismus, Nationalismus, Kosmopolitismus, Dekadenz
are the words repeated over and over
by the artist Hanne Darboven
whose great work in the Hamburger Bahnhof
museum of contemporary art
like the nearby Moabit Prison Memorial
reduces what she knew
to the minimal utterances
the obsessive reductions
the repetitions
that anticipate the ghosts of themselves
in the silence of the archive.

28

'Kropotkin-Vodka'
was the title of the Pussy Riot song that came to mind
by the overflowing rubbish bins and empty bottles
near the Russian War Memorial in Treptower Park
where I hoped some twenty-first-century Proudhonists
might have been partying overnight
in honour of Peter Kropotkin
whose unbending anarchist principles
were a few clicks to the left
of Sozialdemokrat Johannes Wedde.

I like to imagine
that my distant relative's presence as a German delegate
at the First Congress of the Second International
in Paris in 1889
was noted by Kropotkin
on account of the exclusion of anarcho-syndicalists from the
       congress
a remit supported by the 'German Marxists'.

Little did Kropotkin know
while sucking angry spit from his beard
in Bromley High Street, Greater London
that his place of exile would one day
add Siouxsie Sioux and Poly Styrene to its alumni
thus stitching together another of those
'webs of significance'
since both punk singers are cited as role models
by Pussy Riot.

The grim parterre of the war memorial
the aggrandising monumentality of its architecture

the bad faith of its lugubrious statues
and fatuous bas-relief narratives
were deserving of an anarchic Pussy Riot party
but I had to make do with the underground moles
whose modest subversions
had built memorial-mounds across the picnic-grounds
of Treptower Park.

Little homages to peaceful coexistence
to which I later raised a glass of icy Stoli
during the din of happy hour
at the Kino bar on the corner.

29

Johannes Wedde. Gedenkblätter von seiner Schwester
(Hermann Grüning, Hamburg 1891) –

A year after his death in 1890
the asthmatic little firebrand's beloved sister and housemate
Theodora Frueherer Wedde
published the 'commemorative pages'
a biography of her brother with extracts from his writing
in which the small world of a household
might seem the metonym of a larger one
liebenswürdig und geistvoll
'amiable and witty'
the terms used by Wilhelm Blos
to describe the sister
to whom Johannes dedicated a poem
An Theodora Wedde
Als Dank für Geschenk einer Traube
'To Theodora Wedde
As Thanks for the Gift of a Grape'
am ersten des Weinmonds
on the first day of October's grape harvest, 1877
thanking his *freundliche Bakchantin*
for the gift of wine

with which they may have toasted
the martyrs of the 1871 Paris Commune
commemorated by Johannes
in his poem 'Zum Gedächtnis' (1876).

The record shows
that only thirteen copies of the *Gedenblätter*
are held in libraries worldwide.

The record of the Commune martyrs
is also frugal
and might be summed up in the phrase
stimmt so – keep the change.

The small change of memory.
History's emolument.

30

Walle, Regen, walle nieder,
Wecke meine alten Lieder,
Die wir in der Türe sangen,
Wie die Tropfen draussen klangen!

'Pour, rain, pour down,
Awaken my old songs,
Which we sang in the doorway,
When the drops rang outside!'

The Brahms setting of 'Regenlied'
received by the poet Klaus Groth in 1873
is said to have had an emotional effect on Clara Schumann
though which of the words or the music
moved her more
is a subversive question at best
since she knew well enough
that when Klaus wrote of raindrops falling
tears would usually follow

as melancholia may follow memory
and not least the memory of her husband
poor Robert Schumann
dead at forty-six
speechless but sung to by angels.

31

Schweiss und Blut
But when Johannes Wedde writes of 'sweat and blood' falling
rather than raindrops
in his panegyric to the Paris Commune martyrs of 1871
he anticipates an awakening
'in the fresh bosom of youth'.

He drives memory forward into hope
Groth backward into melancholy.

Johannes looks outward to the future
Klaus inward to the past.

They are the antiphonal ghosts
that sing to me
'Some days chicken salad
some days chicken shit.'

And then on a warm evening
nine going on ten
the light fading
Boxhagener Park full of people with dogs and children
a punk girl band singing a cover of
'Day that Time Forgot'
just shutting the ghosts up.

32

immer nur meine Eintönigkeit,
mein Schattenzwang
(Gottfried Benn) –

'only my own monotony always,
my coactive shadows'
is what I'm stuck with
from my morning's reading
which I haven't escaped
by riding my bike into the Plänterwald
and stopping on the riverbank
across from the Rummelsburg power plant
near a fisherman
whose float bobbing on the placid Spree
predictably reminds me
of my own hope
that before long
a word will
tug my line.

The power plant's vapourising breath
seems to have been painted against the sky

the efflatus of power
that should evaporate as a matter of course
being no more than a residue
but cannot
and hangs there motionlessly.

Once it's clear that the fisherman
is content to feed fish not catch them

I ride home
accompanied necessarily
by my coactive shadow.

33

. . . politisch ohne Vorurteil
'political without prejudice'
was how Johannes Wedde
'Redakteur der "Burger Zeitung" in Hamburg'
had described a friend of his
a local merchant
in a letter to Friedrich Engels in London
which Engels had quoted in his letter
to the Italian socialist Pascale Martignetti
('London, 21. Mai 1887')
passing on (from Johannes Wedde)
the merchant Johannes Paul's request
for a photograph of Martignetti
adding
that the situation for socialists in Hamburg
was getting worse by the day
and further (however)
that his (Engels's) eye was getting better
wie es scheint
(so it seems)
but that serious work was out of the question
and that included 'Ihr Manuskript'
Martignetti's translation of Marx's essay on
subcontracting and capital.

I pause to brew coffee
and empty my mind of this historical clutter.

Outside the kitchen window
sunshine variegates the flickering pale greens
of the freshly unfurled five-fingered chestnut tree leaves
that now conceal the nest

the Elster have finished reinforcing
where they will soon raise their family.

I watch them come and go
but the nest I can't see
has moved into my mind
a 'coactive shadow'
a ghost
sharing space with the mysterious photograph
of the Italian Pascale Martignetti
negotiated via Engels by my busy cousin
on behalf of his friend in Hamburg.

Was the man fishing in the Spree
the ghost of my great-grandfather Heinrich August?

The ghosts are in my mind
but don't know they are
which is why I don't believe them
which is why the fisherman
gazing at the river's glittering opacity
opposite the Rummelsburg power plant
didn't turn and address me
in the Plattdüütsch
with which he might have uttered
a final curse
as the cold water of the Wairau River
smacked him in his Hun face
before filling his lungs
that had sucked up the thick fog
off Punta Arenas
the saltmarshy breezes of Poitou-Charentes
and the blustering seaspray of the Karori Rip

when his shipmates knew him as
Heinrich August Wedde
with one leg crooked from a badly set fracture
and rumour had it
with something crooked in his past also
but not as crooked as the corner he turned
and was lost to sight
in a future somewhere south-east of Sydney.

Someone struck his name off the crew list.

Now it comes to mind.

34

The sadness was form, the happiness content.
Happiness filled the space of sadness.
I wasn't thinking about Milan Kundera's unforgettable aphorism
as I sat in late afternoon sunshine
on the corner by the Kino bar
fishing the fluffy Linden blossoms out of my beer

but about my great-grandmother Maria
a little haunting that made my heart ache.

The ache came back again the next morning
along with Kundera's aperçu
as I drank my coffee by the open kitchen window
after a shower of rain
had made the chestnut tree's heavy leaves
droop their five fingers languorously
in the still air.

First the casting away of leaves in autumn
then the casting of twiggy shadows
the casting of blossom
of shade.

And again
and again.

What did Maria cast away
looking out the draughty window
in Bute Street, Wellington
at the obdurate evergreen of taupata
and those 'cabbage trees'
those sky-mops?

And was it happiness
that filled the space
her sadness had made for it?

35

'Look at life with the eyes of a child'
advised the great artist Käthe Kollwitz
who took as her subjects
the victims of poverty, hunger and war.

My great-grandmother Maria Reepen's grandmother
was born Wiebke Claussen in 1775
a Danish patronymic
her mother was Elisabeth Peters
North German patronymic
born about 1824
on the fractious Baltic borders
and her sisters were
Eliese (1836)
Sophie (1838)
Charlotte (1842)
Amelia (1846)
Elisabeth (1855)
her brothers
Heinrich (1840)
Johannes (1848)
Konrad (1853)

Droning black bees in early summer
was what they'd have seen
around the chestnut and linden trees of Kiel
and in the wild grasses of the ländlichen Gaarden
overlooking the busy Kieler Hafen Förde.

Swarms of black smoke
about the fortifications of Dybbøl
in the terrible winter of 1864

when the Prussians crushed Denmark
was what Maria's brothers may have seen
across the frozen marshes.

Not seen by my great aunts and uncles
the smoke of Kiel burning

4000 tonnes of bombs
9 April 1941
3 August 1941
14 May 1943
13 December 1943
21 January 1944
24 July 1944
16/17 August 1944
27 August 1944
15/16 September 1944
9 April 1945
14 April 1945
3 May 1945

But by their children perhaps
or children's children
those that stayed and saw
the droning swarms above Kieler Hafen.

36

Würde Welt plötzlich anders,
wir weinten
(Ernst Meister) –

'Were the world suddenly changed
we would weep.'

But not perhaps
if what changed was Käthe Kollwitz's law of wars
that 'every war already carries within
the war which will answer it' –

her son
Peter Kollwitz
dead at eighteen
on the Western Front 1914
her grandson
Peter Kollwitz
on the Russian Front 1942.

37

Mit Heimweh und Brechreiz beladene Schiffe
(Günter Grass) –

'Ships laden with homesickness and seasickness'
is how we might picture
the emigrant vessels that left Hamburg's
'port of dreams'

but what if Maria Reepen at twenty-four
had already lived with the Danish wars
and foresaw others

saw *die adelige Preussen Offizieren*
the noble Prussian officers
in their pomp
by Kieler Schloss

had seen the tall ships entering Kieler Hafen
their crews coming ashore
with tattoos
new languages
giant conches and fine porcelain
a Māori patu

and tall stories that grew taller in the telling
along chilly Schönbergerstraße
where horses lost their footing on frozen snow
and a crowd of children stood in the road
looking back down the hill

one young housemaid leaning on a fence railing
in her soiled white apron.

38
We are not desperate idiots of history
(Rudi Dutschke) –

I'm thinking about this
while sitting by the kitchen window
drinking Ruth Hennrich's 'Guten Morgen' tea
from her stall in the Saturday market
(Brennessel, Minze, Rosen, Mate, Hibiskus, Zitronen-Verbene)

bored by my late start
and yes
a little hungover perhaps
or it could be the spring pollen.

I look out at the chestnut tree
its five-fingered leaves languorous
and its flower-towers weary
after a fall of rain.

It already seems to be
the endlessly recursive
'coactive shadow'

or ghost
of itself.

The Elsters' twiggy nest a memory phantom
obscured by repetition.

The black cat slips across dappled shadows
again.

On the other side of the courtyard
Werther and Lotte
nod and coo to each other
repetitively
on a window ledge
while a child presses her face to the windowpane –
dicht und schön
no doubt.

The crazy guy strides along Grünbergerstraße
shouting 'Fuck Nazis! Fuck capitalism!'
while people go past on bikes
in both directions
(they've seen him before).

Little children in brightly coloured hoodies
walk hand in hand to Boxhagener Park
and back.

Doug comes by with his son Huw
and we go to visit Rudi Dutschke's grave
out at Sankt-Annen in Dahlem.

'We can change.
We are not desperate idiots of history
unable to take their destiny in their own hands.'

Happy Birthday, Rudi
(born March 7, 1940).

Sorry we're a bit late
but never too.

39

'Your eloquence is in your lips.'
Easter Monday breakfast
on the pavement outside the Blattwerk Blumenhandlung
was with my florist neighbours Klaus, Petra, Melanie and Jessie

who know me for what I am
and whose hospitality is inversely proportional to my transience
and my halting German
which
having exhausted the conversational topics
of my Schleswig-Holsteine or perhaps dänishe Urgroßmutter
my deutsch or perhaps polnisch Urgroßvater
the talents of my wife Donna
(whom they eagerly hoped to meet)
and
(with some patience)
the question of what is Germany's future

I was dismissed with a tolerant smile
while the table turned its attention
to topics that made them laugh

which they continued to do while waving
as I passed them on my bicycle
heading for the Schoenbrunn Biergarten
in the Friedrichshain Volkspark
by way of Straße der Pariser Kommune
known as Fruchtstraße until March 17, 1971
when it was renamed to commemorate
the 100th anniversary of the Paris Commune

a topic of conversation
that excited my distant relative Johannes Wedde
in his 1876 poem 'Zum Gedächtnis'
that in his mind
as well as being *in memoriam*
spoke to 'the future of Germany'

where I sat down in my silent presence
as language formed a frothing head above my thoughts
and an American casting agent at the next table
reassured a German actress
who was about to be dubbed.

'Don't worry
your eloquence is in your lips.'

Which were distended with dermal filler.

Later
I sat under a profusely flowering lilac
in Boxhagener Park
where Easter Monday picnics continued into dusk
a child in the playground
demanded to be swung sideways
the sparrows took dust-baths

and I entered the space of dubbed eloquence
my eyes not meeting another's
understanding fragments of language
but not the laughter that gave them futures

a social silence
materialised in the foreign guest's
over-eager deportment at table
or in the firmness of my great-grandmother's posture
her resolute half smile
her gaze that avoided the camera
looking past it to a time
when she will speak for herself.

40

Nur eine einzige Kopie bitte
'Just one only copy please'

sounds original
every time I say it
but then the obedient
the coactive
paradox
naturally follows.

Coming home from the Kopieercentrum
the copy of Johannes Wedde's Paris Commune poem in my bag
I pass a mature dog
holding a puppy's lead in its mouth
and seeming to grin
around the tether.

I read my ancestor's poem by my kitchen window
while drinking a glass of wine.

When I don't understand words
I look out at the chestnut tree
its louche drooping leaves
erect blossom stems
but the whole mass
heaving under the soaking weight
of its future.

Dislodged by the passing shower
its flowers float through hot air.

Bees waver through steamy shafts of sunlight
and settle on the blue flowers of the rosemary plant
in my balcony herb-garden
where I take my wine
and listen to laughter down in the street.

Petersilie
Basilicum
Minze
Thymian
Rosmarin
Oregano
Lavendel

I imagine Maria's firm lips
copying their names
in English

and her laughter
even.

41

'It's so German today,'
says the German woman
in English
to another German woman
sitting beside her on the bench I'm sharing with them
in Boxhagener Park
while I open my notebook and write
It's so German today.

At the fleamarket last Sunday
I could have bought the complete works of Gottfried Benn
in six volumes (€30)
but instead bought a bike for Donna
(same price).

We'll ride along the Spree *am Plänterwald*
where the ghost of Heinrich August
will ignore us
much as the fish ignore his bait

much as Boxhagener Park is ignoring
the sounds of history
across the Oberbaumbrücke
the May Day party at Kottbusser Tor.

'Family friendly,'
says the woman next to me.

'No one is burning cars anymore.'

42

Im Hochsommer besuchen die Bienen
viele unterschiedliche Blüten
comes back to mind
in summer

people dipping their tongues into ice creams
while looking at the sign in the secondhand bookshop's
empty window

Es ist vorbei
it's finished

but thanking loyal customers for their
'always interesting and refreshing conversations

which happen
because we have books

and which are not forgotten.'

43

Bis später
'See you later.'

The joyful acrobatics of swallows
in hot updraughts
as light fades from the cyan sky
between nine and ten in the evening

and the volume of restaurant conversation builds
under the bird-loud lindens.

44

Arbeiter-und Bauern-Macht
Expropriated for the enjoyment of citizens
on the principle of
'worker and peasant power'
or the 'dictatorship of the proletariat'

ending the privilege that devolved by stages
from the ancient regime's Count Albrecht Friedrich of
       Brandenburg-Schwedt
but remains inscribed
in the formal parterre of Peter Joseph Lenné

the broad pathways of Tierpark Berlin
on the former grounds of Friedrichsfelde Palace
flicker with the filigreed leaf-patterns
of summer sunlight among trees
through which
accompanied by their fragmented shadows
young mothers and fathers
trundle the zoo's Kinderwagen
as if across an unsteady newsreel screen
from 1955
in which the beneficiaries of GDR policy
which mistrusted a distinction between 'state' and 'society'
enjoyed recreational access
to the docile creatures of the zoo

a metonym of confinement
haunting the cheerful chatter
of the reunified present
the moated vistas of pleasant parkland

inhabited by shaggy Siberian musk-oxen
and louche kangaroos

and
hidden down a prohibited side-track
the nightmarish marabou stork
carrion scavenger
corpse-gorger
crowned with clotted blood

alive and real in the now
and
I imagine
tugging out the toothsome
guts of capital.

45

Nature herself is sublimely eloquent
(Alexander von Humboldt) –

The unlit storage rooms
on the unvisited upper floor
of Berlin's Museum für Naturkunde
are haunted by the dark silhouettes
of taxidermied birds and animals

eyeless and immobile
a vitrine horizon of crests
and upright ears
that seem perpetually alert

sad little ghosts

not dead

just waiting.

46

Humboldt-Universität zu Berlin
an institute of 'higher learning'
sustains the holistic approach to knowledge
established by its illustrious founder
Wilhelm von Humboldt
brother of Alexander

having 'got past'
its National Socialism fervour of 1933–1945
('the most reprehensible period in its history')
and subsequently
in the dainty language of its prospectus
'the influence of the higher education reforms in the GDR'.

In Görlitzer Park
on a hot weekday afternoon
the bored but cheerful drug dealers ply their trade
while a talkative Turkish family barbecues
on one side
acrobats do planking moves on the other
kids ride their bikes through the middle
on the way home from school
and at the Biergarten
drinkers in deckchairs
close their eyes
and smile at futures
projected onto minds
from which memory seems to have been
temporarily erased.

47
Weh mir!
exclaimed Friedrich Hölderlin
in *Wie wenn am Feiertage*
('As on a holiday')
1799

'Woe is me!'
or perhaps
'My shame . . .'

but he couldn't finish it

and in *Hyperion*
Ich kann den Unterschied nicht leiden,
der zwischen uns ist –
'I can't bear the difference
that is between us – '

The story is in the word *Weh*
which means 'ache'
or in *wehtun* which means 'to hurt'
but whose coactive shadow is the word *weg*
which means 'away'
and so I imagine
'to hurt by casting away'

perhaps to a place
where the hurt is of glances not returned
der Unterschied
the difference
the casting away

the irreconcilable trauma
of poor Hölderlin's madness.

But in photographs of her
it's my great-grandmother Maria's direct look
that Donna and I see everywhere in Berlin
especially *am Friedrichshain*
our home for now
and saw up north around Kiel
those clear Baltic eyes
waiting for you to meet them
for *correspondence*

so that language could close the gap of *Wehtun*
a hawser hauled taut
a docking

and if Maria felt the ache of difference
of the hurtful space between
of the look not returned or met
on the streets of Wellington
in 1876
I don't see it in the photographs of her

but feel it in myself
that little ache
as if passing her in Bute Street, Wellington
in 1876
I'd looked away
thinking *different*
and felt her unperturbed gaze
move beyond place into time
without looking back.

48

Hamburger Passagierlisten

Name: Maria Josephin Repen

Departure Date: 6 Okt 1875

Destination: Neuseeland

Birth Date: abt 1851

Age: 24

Gender: weiblich

Residence: Hadersleben, Schleswig

Occupation: Dienstmädchen

Ship Name: Shakespeare

Captain: Jörgensen

Shipping line: Rob. M. Sloman & Co.

Shipping Clerk: C. A. Mathei

Ship Type: Segelschiff

Accommodation: ohne Angabe

Ship Flag: Deutschland

Port of Departure: Hamburg

Port of Arrival: Wellington; Neu Seeland

Source Citation: Staatsarchiv Hamburg; Hamburg,

Deutschland; Hamburger Passagierlisten; Volume: 373-7 I,
    VIII A 1

Band 032 C; Page: 595; Microfilm No.: K_1721.

49

Kiel von seiner Schönsten Seite!
'Kiel by its most beautiful aspect'
is promised by the SFK-Fördetörn ferry
during festive Kielwoche

a round trip taking in the tall ships
the cruise liners
the charming beach resort at Laboe Brücke.

My great-grandfather's windcheater
has the number 5 on its back
on its sleeves the logos
of the 2002 Volvo Ocean Race Around the World
and of some faded Baltic yacht squadrons
and the severed head of John the Baptist
in a chalice
above the name Koszalin.

His bald patch is the colour of a mahogany hatch-cover
his eyes of the sea beyond Sandstrand Falckenstein
his hair of salt-soiled canvas.

His beard flutters in the chilly breeze
where he smokes a Marlboro filter-tip
at the ferry's rail

and wrinkles his eyes
at the ThyssenKrupp Marine Systems submarine boatyard
its HDW Class 216
'predestined for
Anti-surface and anti-submarine warfare

ISTAR – Intelligence, surveillance, target acquisition and
        reconnaissance
Land attack capability
Special Forces operations
Deployment of unmanned vehicles
Mine operations and mine reconnaissance'.

Cigarette butt spat astern.

His glare at me
shows the crooked top tooth we share

his curse
a scornful gull-squawk in the ferry's wake.

50

'Can the present disown the past?'
'No, because it's always too late – '
was the conversation
I thought I overheard
in the Ratsdienergarten von Kiel
where the statue by Heinrich Mißfeldt of my distant cousin
the Plattdüütsch poet Klaus Groth
looks out from his lichened plinth
at the wind-ruffled water of Kleiner Kiel lake.

But the two guys sleeping rough
in the little park
were speaking a funny kind of German
while sharing a bottle of cheap peach Schnapps
and were more likely discussing
if it was time to get another.

Their kits were rolled neatly
to one side of the water-stained pediment
on which scenes from the Plattdüütsch poems
for which Groth is remembered
were depicted in bas-relief
together with parallel translations
in the Hochdeutsch for which he was forgotten.

His *Hundert Blätter*
scattered into a past
like leaves from his pleasant park
among the lake's fussy ducks.

51

*I didn't know I loved so many things and I had to wait until sixty
to find it out sitting by the window on the Prague–Berlin train
watching the world disappear as if on a journey of no return*
(Nâzim Hikmet Ran, 19 April 1962) –

Polish French and Georgian in his ancestry
Turkish in his language
Communist in his heart
dead in exile in Moscow June 1963
fêted no doubt in East Berlin in 1962

and I saw his ghost on Oranienstraße in Kreuzberg
on a hot Berlin evening in July 2014.

Police had cordoned off the rowdy demonstration
in support of immigrants
near Görlitzer Park
but in nearby Oranienstraße
the footpath was crowded with chairs and tables
and Hikmet was sitting there
with a bunch of male friends
drinking a glass of tea
somewhat daintily eating slices of melon with cheese

and while chewing
was holding the empty fork by his right ear
as if listening to the perfect pitch of exile
a tone found somewhere in the chord combining
the demonstrators over at Wienerstraße
the expostulations of his Turkish companions
and the voice of the German soccer commentator

on the café's big screen
calling the quarter-final
between Germany and France.

52

Tahir, Taksim, Tempelhof:
Das Feld gehört uns allen!
Tahir Square in Egypt
Taksim Square in Turkey
Tempelhofer Feld in Berlin:
'The field belongs to us all!'

Held by Donna's hand
and by her smile also
Mario's twilight kite
dips in salutation
above the family barbecues of Neukölln
the trendy runway skaters
the drinking-game students
those who voted for the *Feld*

and 298 wild bee species
sharing the grassland commune
with nesting larks.

53

der Narzißmus der kleinen Differenzen
'. . . the narcissism of small differences . . .'

What Freud meant is clear
but what's implied is
that the small difference
may point to a large one
for example the thick-browed bureaucratic *Nationalismus*
of the bored pedant
at the Ausgabeort of the Staatsbibliothek
in Potsdamerstraße
where I went with an excited heart
to collect the second volume of Johannes Wedde's
Gesammelte Werke (Hermann Grünig, Hamburg 1894)
in order to read his poem 'Zum Gedächtnis' (Hamburg 1876)
my fiery relative's impassioned paean
in memory of the last battle of the 1871 Paris Commune
'am Kirchhof Père La Chaise'.

Failing to find it in the loan stacks
I said to the narcissist of small differences
as he glared at this Ausländer
across his Ausgabeort barrier
Ich kann den Buch nicht finden
at which
having got it
he pushed the book against my chest
and jeered
Hier ist der Buch!

Books are *das* not *der*
an error I hope Johannes will humour

since the record shows
I'm the first person to open his book
in one hundred and eleven years
and since he greets me
An meine Leser!
with a comradely exclamation mark
above the inked Besitzstempel
Ex Biblioth. Regia Berolinensi 1903.

And also since it was in 1876
the year of 'Zum Gedächtnis'
that Maria Reepen stepped ashore in Wellington
bringing little of her country with her
except her Gedächtnis
her memory of it

and those differences grammar reduces
to the petty narcissisms of nationalist bigots
whose gazes wouldn't meet hers
across *der Unterschied.*

Unheimlich.

Talks funny.

54

'I think I'll let it go'
is what my great-uncle Frederic Alexander Wedde
known as Fritz
the sixth of Maria's eight children
is reported to have said
by S. Dutton-Pegram
the British Vice-Consul in Torreon Mexico
when told that making a will would cost him $10

meaning either that he was stingy
or that he'd drifted beyond the reach of Gedächtnis
and beyond the thoughts of his seven siblings
and of his nieces and nephews
who might have benefitted from a will
including my father Frederick Albert Wedde
who shared his uncle's initials
as well as his wandering ways.

The 1875 Hamburg passenger list of Fritz's mother
my father's grandmother
Maria Reepen
lists Hadersleben (in German) as her place of residence
Haderslev (in Danish)
a town passed back and forth
between the Duchy of Schleswig
a Danish fief
and after the Second Schleswig War in 1864
Prussia and the North German Confederation
and from 1871 the German Empire
later returned to Denmark
by the Schleswig Plebiscite of 1920
seven years before Maria died

on 12 June in Kaitieke New Zealand
it's said while reciting poetry
whether in Danish or German
is not within reach of the family's Gedächtnis
and was buried on 14 June 1927 in Raurimu Cemetery
near the backblocks farm
where she ended her days.

She left Hamburg in 1875
but when did she leave Kiel
her birthplace and the home of her family
and go to Haderslev in Denmark?

Her sixth child Fritz left Sydney on the *Guthrie*
bound for Singapore
30 June 1906
and wasn't heard of for fifty years.

He died intestate in his Mexican 'observatory'
leaving easy pickings for the lawyers of Torreón
and Eagle Pass Texas
as well as a terse document
'A New Hypothesis or Theory of the Universe'
in which
above his admonition
'Please keep this paper
as it may be of interest sometime in the future'
I encounter the succinct ghost of his thought

that there are spaces between us
like those between the astronomical bodies
he gazed at in Torreón Mexico's
clear desert sky

traversed by memory as if by light
a force-field at once fixed and
as it were
intestate.

55
dein letztes Werk
'your latest work'
(*Vier ernste Gesänge*)
was what Klaus Groth thanked Johannes Brahms for
in a letter of September 1896
not knowing but guessing perhaps
that *letztes* might also mean 'last'
Brahms dead in Vienna April 3 1897.

Out of the silence that filled Kiel
which resembled the silence of the tall ships
moving like swans without visible effort
down Kieler Hafen Förde

a silence that seemed to empty time from space

once Kielwoche's soundstages were gone
the KrautRock one in the Alter Markt
rattling the windows of Nikolaikirche
big band from the naval base at Tirpitzhafen
playing swing in the Rathausplatz
and the Shanty Chor of aged Matrose in period sailor-suits
getting the crowd singing and swaying
at the stage down by the station

late at night

after Germany had taken the game 2–1 against Algeria
'in extra time'

and when the town itself
seemed to have been emptied of time

along with the populace that counted time
with its breathing

came the sound of a piano
across the deserted street
and through our hotel room's open window.

I think it was one of the 'Six Little Preludes'
pedagogical pieces by Johann Sebastian Bach
short learning exercises
to be repeated over and over

as perhaps they were by Doris Groth
wife of the Plattdüütsch poet

patiently
taking her time
her fingers returning to begin again
and again
on the Blüthner grand
turning time back
at the house in the Schwanenweg
where she and her husband would play
four-hand arrangements
of the late string quartets of Beethoven

the Blüthner keys visited also by Clara Schumann
Hans von Bülow
and Johannes Brahms
and by the family's friend Dr. Theodor Thomsen
a fluent accompanist for Julius Stockhausen.

Or perhaps she
is warming up
while waiting for her friend Dr. Thomsen
with whom she
will play
the Brahms setting
of Symphony no. 3 (Arrangement for piano four-hands)
    F Major Op. 90
written in the summer of 1883
at Wiesbaden

Klaus listening from his study
die Kajüte (the cabin)
with its door open to the garden.

Seagulls.
Children.

But
Doris Groth dead in January 1878
five years before the Wiesbaden Third
the Blüthner not opened for a year
the wounding letter from Brahms
('you know nothing about music')
repeating itself in the silence
that his wife had filled with her time.

56

Es ist vorbei . . . es ist nie vorbei!
After visiting the Käthe Kollwitz Museum
in salubrious Fasanenstraße
I sat in the sun-dappled garden of the next-door Literaturhaus
drinking a cup of Sommerbeeren tea
while assiduous bees worked the flowerbeds
and writers their Kaffee und Kuchen guests

and was grateful for
the crazy guy in a yellow visibility jerkin
who read aloud from his manuscript novel
hundreds of pages
on which he'd typed
'It's over . . . it's never over'

over and over.

57

Wir bitten um Geduld bis Ihre Nummer
in der Anzeige erscheint.
Danke!
In Haus C-Z3
Room 26
at the Ausländerbehörde on Friedrich-Krause-Ufer
over the road from the murky water
of the Berlin-Spandauer-Schifffahrtskanal
in which the ThyssenKrupp metal works are reflected
we sit patiently as requested
for Donna's number 115 to appear.

The waiting room of those desiring visas
and to live safely in peace with their families in Berlin
is harangued by a madman
while at the interview counter
a proud boy translates German for his grandfather

a young mother shovels noodles into her son's mouth
(he sings sweetly between swallows)

a pale guy doodles
then falls asleep with a rapt smile on his face

a young couple with matching capped teeth
exchange flirty looks
transforming C-Z3 26 into a bedroom
while the sun shines on the outside world

a little girl drapes her skinny arm
over her father's large stomach

a young mullah joins a man preparing to pray
having bathed his feet in the washroom

people's thoughts turn inward
the way their eyes are looking
dazed and resigned

half a dozen languages
at least

every kind of shoe

and
'I love this shit!'
yells the madman
as security arrives.

Leaving Haus C-Z3 with Donna's visa
we pass a man
desperately sobbing.

58

Er ist eigentlich dumm aber auch irgendwie nicht
(Hannah Arendt) –

'He is actually stupid, but then, somehow, he is not,'
wrote Hannah Arendt to Karl Jaspers
Jerusalem 1961
from the trial of SS-Obersturmbannführer Adolf Eichmann
whose presence at the Wannsee Conference
20 January 1942
on the shores of the placid Großer Wannsee
expedited 'Operation Reinhardt'
the 'Final Solution'
named in memory of SS-Obergruppenführer Reinhard
         Heydrich.

We bike past 56–58 Am Großen Wannsee
in order to swim in the warm lake at Große Tiefehorn
and celebrate our wedding anniversary
with fresh strawberries and cream
and a glass of rosé
by the ferry to Pfaueninsel

and pass the villa again
on the way back

through the implacable conduit
where Arendt disciplined her bafflement
into thought
and her thought into the question of how to understand
what it means to be at home in the world.

A question asked also
by the Stolpersteine
the 'stumbling block' cobblestones
in memory of murdered Jews
that we pass daily in Niederbarnimstraße
as do the chattering cavalcades of children
from the neighbourhood Kita
making their way to sunny Boxhagener Park.

59

'The banality of evil'
a phrase for which Arendt was castigated
after publishing *Eichmann in Jerusalem*
aptly describes the watering can
fitted with a hidden camera
with which to spy on cemetery visitors

now on display in the Stasi Museum
Haus 1 of the former headquarters
of the DDR-Staatssicherheit
in the working-class Berlin suburb of Lichtenberg
whose traces of socialist optimism
have become as hard to decipher
as the stupidity of the bugged watering-can.

60

$\underline{p}$ á $\underline{ci}$

venez   *sans*

wrote 'Frederick the Great' to his house-guest Voltaire
some time between 1750 and 1753
to which the philosopher replied

G   *a*

(*Venez sous p à sans sous ci*)
(*Gé-grand a-petit*)

('Come and dine at Sans Souci.')
('I have a big appetite.')

The 'philosopher king'
Friedrich II
King of Prussia and Elector of Brandenburg
and the sceptical *philosophe*
despite some testy moments
relished each other's witty company
as well as the fruits vegetables and wines
of the king's estates
at Sanssouci near Potsdam

these days a popular tourist destination
whose name 'no worries'
accompanies the visitor
through the elaborate 'Frederician Rococo'
of the summer palace

and whose carefree ambience casts a discreet veil
over the King's military and imperialist accomplishments
not least the 'Germanisation' of Poland in the 1770s
execrated by the doubter Voltaire
but admired by the Nazis
a century and a half later.

Among the splendours of the art collection
in the Picture Gallery designed by 'Old Fritz' himself
and built 'under the supervision' of Johann Gottfried Büring
the awe-struck visitor will find
Caravaggio's *Incredulità di San Tommaso* (1601–02)
in which Doubting Thomas
permits his index finger to be inserted
between the fleshy lips
of an open wound.

61

Solch ein Gewimmel möcht' ich sehn,
Auf freiem Grund mit Freien Volke stehn.
(Goethe, *Faust*) −

The ecstasies of swallows
hot-air-surfing at dusk
above Hermann Henselmann's apartments
'Highrise on the Weavers' Meadow'
in Karl Marx Allee

may have cheered the weary men and women
the bricklayers and *die Trümmerfrauen*
the builders and the rubble-clearers
who volunteered their labour
to build the 'Workers' Palaces'
clad in Meissen porcelain tiles
and decorated with bas-reliefs
wrought iron gates
and mosaics

not the frivolity of 'Frederician Rococo'
but in their own way
expressing belief
in a care-free society

the monumental 'National Construction Tradition'
looking in one direction at the Stalinist 'Seven Sisters' of
        Moscow
and in the other
at the Prussian pomp
of Karl Friedrich Schinkel

a dialectical aesthetic
one might say
partially restored
by the West German investment bank
that bought the dilapidated dream street
when the Wall came down
with an eye to its commercial restoration
(the money ran out)

and
perhaps
with some consideration for the inscription
on the façade of the Haus des Kindes
19 Strausberger Platz am Karl Marx Allee
in which Goethe hopes to see 'a crowd of free people
standing on freedom's soil'

a hope audiences shared
during sixty performances of *Faust* in 1912
at the Rose Theatre
in working-class Friedrichshain
where No. 80 Karl Marx Allee now stands
on the space cleared of its war rubble

and the dream likewise
of my esteemed *Vetter*
the Sozialdemokrat Johannes Wedde
and of my great-grandfather Heinrich August Wedde
turning well-thumbed pages of *Faust*
my father remembered him reading aloud
in his bed at York Terrace, Blenheim
before closing his copy for the last time
in 1915

an 'enemy alien'
in the minds of some townsfolk.

62

Life goes on
sang the Chills
their encore
at the Lido in Kreuzberg
on a stinking hot night in late July
having closed the set with
'Pink Frost':

'I'm really not lying
I'm so scared.'

Which is what the drunk
on the number 10 tram along rowdy Warschauerstraße
seemed to be saying
to his attentive dog
which registered its own existential bafflement
along with its love for the drunk
by the way it tilted its head
from side to side
while blinking its one good eye.

63

I'm so scared
antiphon to the Chills'
'Life goes on'

the familiar dialectic
between quotidian and terror

'banal' even

the dawn beak-clatter and grawk
of the Elster young
in their shady chestnut tree nest
outside our bedroom window
where later their parents peaceably preen
side by side

in the dappled sunlight

that edits bee flights

into the flicker of missile
trajectories
'homing in'.

64

Es ist Zeit, daß es Zeit wird.
When Paul Celan wrote
'It's time it were time'
he concluded by adding
'It is time.'

The punks 'with time on their hands'
by the four fountains
in the grassy strip along Frankfurter Allee
opposite the Pablo-Neruda-Bibliothek
ignore their dogs
(which are entertaining themselves in the fountains)
while sharing a crate of cheap Berliner Pilsener
and a joint or two

and greeting the elderly residents
from the retirement Hinterhäuser
who also encourage their dogs
to play in the fountains
while they
(the elderly residents)
pause for a cigarette
and a chat with the punks

before pushing their walking frames
towards a future
that at times
seems a thing of the past.

65

Wenn die Ideen begraben sind
Kommen die Knochen heraus
(Volker Braun) –

'When ideas are buried
The bones emerge'

All afternoon
the storm held off
or
'time stood still'.

Faces along '2.2 kilometres' of Karl Marx Allee
at the Berliner Bierfestival
reddened
as did the sunset.

The smoke of grills
drifted across the flaming windows
of the 'Workers' Palaces'.

A German cover of Megadeath's
'Tornado of Souls'
competed for the attention
of the crowd

among whom could be seen
the Trümmerfrauen ghosts
dancing on the dessicated grass
they'd cleared of rubble
seventy years ago

and of the Staub
that nonetheless returns
after the storm has passed.

66

. . . eine stunde lang war eine
stunde da wo weder du noch ich vorher gewesen war.
(Norbert Hummelt) –

'. . . for more than an hour we were simply
there in an hour where neither you nor I had ever been before.'

The ghosts of meaning
that haunt phenomena

as hard to wave away
as wasps
attracted to the clamped lips
that have sipped wine
and with which I want

to admonish
the coactive shadow
stalking what's
unable to escape
the supplement or surplus
the allegory
the spook
significance

bag chestnut tree bees *Fenster* ice sunsets barbecues
raindrops spring flowers *Staub* photograph nest smoke
cat pigeon lips swallows zoo submarine cigarette lake
park kite observatory seagulls children sunset wine
shoes strawberries camera wound dusk rubble dog
missile storm

coopted into séance
where ghosts
are the words with which things
utter themselves

woo hoo

the mad ontological ranting
of what's always coming
to an end

but never does.

67

In jedem Werk gibt es die Stelle, an der es uns kühl anweht
wie die kommende Frühe.
(Volker Braun) –

'In every work, there is that spot where we feel a gust of cold,
like the dawn, coming.'

In mid summer
the sticky bill-stickers go by on their bikes

and the five-fingered leaves of the chestnut tree
are turning brown
where the falling blossoms
stuck to them
in late spring

as if postering
the autumn programme.

68

Woo-hoo-hoo-hoo
The monotonous woo-hoo-hoo-hooing
of Werther and Lotte
at dawn
4:30am to be precise

and the crashing of the rubbish-bin collection
two hours later

mark the beginning and the end
Anfang und Ende
of a dream
from which I wake and wonder
why
my son Conrad
a musician
has had to rescue me from a house
whose walls are composed of chords
which he parries with one hand
while leading me out with the other

after which he kisses me
and walks away
towards the kitchen
where I am making coffee

and discover that I am awake

and he has gone.

69

'last concert 25 august'
The young guy with blue hair
and a sweet tremulous voice
singing in the forecourt
of the Warschauerstraße U-Bahn
next to a sign that reads
'last concert 25 august'
(eleven sleeps away)
gets my 2-euro coin
and also my silence
in which the word 'Anfang'
longs to be uttered.

On the Landwehrkanal
the La Belle tour-boat glides past
edging the motionless swans aside.

On the sunny banks of the canal
those with little to do
do it.

Something may be imminent
something else ending.

The canal's torpid water
seems to dither between these options.

70

Lecker
is what the day utters
when at four in the afternoon
I go downstairs
get an ice cream across the street
and sit in mild dappled sunlight
hearing the word 'tasty'
on all sides

a complex
and paradoxical pleasure
since *lecker* might equally describe
the twin scoops of Haselnuss-Eis
and the sadness
that has begun to fill my mouth
with the bittersweet words
we use to say goodbye.

71

Endeanfang
The leaves of the lilac in Boxhagener Park
wear the dusty patina
the city *Staub*
that accumulates between thunderstorms.

The lilac's purple blossoms
have long gone
since I sat here in early spring
writing in my notebook
(as now)
as if I was
'making a start'.

The usual affable drunks
are squabbling on the bench to my right
while to my left
an eye-locked couple
move their lips soundlessly
around the word *liebe*.

Then they taste each other's ice creams.

The child who prefers to go sideways on her swing
is at it again.

What did Maria Reepen know she'd miss
when it was time to leave
her familiar plants and seasons
the voices and words
that would replay in her memory

and when the place
where these things made sense
was elsewhere?

72

. . . im Herbstmanöver der Zeit
(Ingeborg Bachmann) –

'In time's autumn manoeuvre'

the delicate blade-shaped linden leaves
begin to spiral down
one by one
and the spatulate
spring-blossom imprinted posters
of the chestnut
will soon keep busy the guys
who sweep around the bikes and rubbish bins
in the courtyard above which
the Hinterhaus's raucous guardians
the Elster and their young
are seldom heard anymore
as though the industrious weeks of spring
and the fractious responsibilities of summer
have fallen away too
into time's holding pattern

and I'm back
where I started
in a place at once familiar
and like nowhere I know

as if to be here ever
I must always leave
without knowing I'll be back.

The sparrows taking dust-baths
in Boxi Park
the kids playing soccer on the grass
the permanent park-bench resident
with his grey-beard dog
library of graphic novels
and schedule of visitors

are becoming

what I've always
never seen before

ghosts not just of themselves
but of the present
in which their time was always passing.

73

Wake up (wake up)
Grab a brush and put a little make-up . . .
(System of a Down) –

On a chilly evening in late August
at club SO36 in Oranienstraße
the pianist Viktoriya Yermolyeva
aka Vika
('Vika Goes Wild')
and her drummer Gabor
shredding System of a Down's
'Chop Suey!'

was . . .

how could that be?

– haunted by Beethoven's
Great Fugue in B flat Major Op. 133
and the unrestrained joy
of Klaus and Doris Groth
riffing for four hands
on Schwanenweg
while fog bells clanged
over on Kieler Hafen Förde.

74

Wie ich das Bild zum Schweigen brachte, 2012

'How I brought the picture to silence'
is only the most obvious translation
of Piotr Nathan's work
at the Halle am Berghain
the decommissioned power station
on the eastern bank of the Spree

in the video component of which the artist
dressed in a white suit
addresses what cannot be uttered
the intoxication of oblivion and disappearance

first ascending a ladder
and painting the word 'Anfang'
in bold white letters
across a grandiose allegory of the primeval

and next
reascending the ladder
and obliterating this 'beginning'
with bold sweeps of white

until he too
seems to disappear
into the silence
of his own erasure.

75

Festival der Riesendrachen auf dem Tempelhofer Feld
The melancholy of transit
seemed to tug at the happy families
enjoying the Tempelhof Festival of Kites

whose distance from the former Columbia-Haus
concentration camp
just across the road
calibrated the *Endeanfang* of a history
in which time is stretched
not broken

and in which the imperturbable swans on the Landwehrkanal
by the Fraenkelufer synagogue
the people having a beer in autumn sunshine
on the nearby bridge at Admiralbrücke
the drug dealers at Kottbusser Tor
and the chestnuts clanging on the roofs
of parked cars

now begin to be attenuated into memory

as we arrive in Auckland
in huckster spring
when the city starts to preen
its fake tan glamour

and the Hauraki Gulf's gusty gale
that would shred the kites over Tempelhof
and tear apart the power plant's
motionless smoke-plume
above the placid Spree

instead scatters fragrant frangipani flowers
on the footpath
just around the corner from our place.

76

Plenitude
the principle of optimism advanced by Gottfried Leibniz
in his *Théodicée* of 1710
and fifty years later
mocked as Panglossianism by Voltaire in *Candide,*
    ou l'Optimisme
must have struck a chord with my great-uncle Fritz
the family's mystery man
a devotee of *Aufklärung*
since by post from Mexico
he sent his nephew
my second cousin Peter
'a two-volume edition of the essays
and shorter writings of Leibniz
modern American translations'.

Fritz's mother
Peter's great-grandmother
my great-grandmother
Maria Josephine Catharina Wedde

buried in Raurimu cemetery
14 June 1927
'last seen alive by certifying doctor' 11 June 1927
'Senile Arteritis – 6 years'
'Coronary Stenosis – 3 days'

'Age of each living daughter – 47 43'
'Age of each living son – 50 48 46 42 39 38'

'Usual occupation, profession or job – Widow'

'Mother:
First/given name(s) – Not Recorded
Surname/family name – Not Recorded
First/given names at birth – Not Recorded
Surname/family name at birth – Not Recorded'

'Father:
First/given name(s) – Johannis
Surname/family name – Reepen'

'Spouse/Partner:
First/given name(s) – August Henry
Surname/family name – Wedde'

Steep 'third class country'
thin volcanic ash soil
on a skiddy greywacke base
that her sons cleared of forest
up in the King Country boondocks

and watched slabs of hill pasture
slide into the creeks.

Maria was celebrated as a seamstress
up there in the back country.

No simpering three-quarter studio profile
in photographs of Maria
and that direct gaze
looking past what was left behind
(her mother's name for instance)
at a future neither fatuously optimistic
nor fatalistically pessimistic

a 'plenitude'
in der besten aller möglichen Welten
the best of all possible worlds

leaving much to be desired
no doubt
but not discouraging her son Fritz from his wanderings
nor her daughters from their learning.

I meant to bring a chestnut
from the path along Fraenkelufer
by the Landwehrkanal in Kreuzberg
where we made our last home in Berlin
and where in early autumn
the kids from the nearby Kita
came in a colourful chattering crocodile
to collect the glossy nuts
in red plastic buckets

because I planned to press a chestnut
into the damp earth
by the grave of my Urgroßmutter
Maria Josephine Catharina Reepen
thinking it might grow into a tree
in der besten aller möglichen Welten

but forgot it

so instead plant in myself the memory
the coactive shadow
the ghost
of the chestnut tree

through which I watched the seasons pass
during which words also came and went
and were sometimes remembered.

Notes

3

'. . . *rocks on the one hand and dreams on the other – they are things of this world.*'

The quote is from 'Thick Description: Toward an Interpretive Theory of Culture', Clifford Geertz's first chapter in *The Interpretation of Cultures* (Basic Books, 1973). The chapter was written last, after the selection of essays was already complete. The term 'thick description', described by Geertz as a borrowed 'notion from Gilbert Ryle', became, Geertz wrote in the Preface to the 2000 edition, 'a position and a slogan I have been living with since'. I have gone on reading and admiring these essays for many years and want to acknowledge that the concept of 'thick description' was my passport to the state of mind I hoped this book would occupy, where ghosts could be encountered in the everyday, material world, and in the phantom fragments of language that seemed to collate its meanings. The extended quote is:

> The thing to ask about a burlesqued wink or a mock sheep raid is not what their ontological status is. It is the same as that of rocks on the one hand and dreams on the other – they are things of this world. (p.10)

5

Min Modersprak, wa klingst du schön! ('My mothertongue, how sweet you sound!')

I first found my distant cousin-of-some-sort Klaus Groth's Platt-düütsch poems at the website lowlands-l.net/groth, where Reinhard Hahn translates 'Modersprak' as 'native tongue', which I have changed. The poem was first published in *Quickborn, Volksleben – in plattdeutschen Gedichten Ditmarscher Mundart* (1852); the 25th edition was published in 1900.

131

6

Von allem Leid, das diesen Bau erfüllt,
Ist unter Mauerwerk und Eisengittern
Ein hauchlebendig, ein geheimes Zittern.

Albrecht Georg Haushofer (7 January 1903–23 April 1945)
was murdered by SS troopers as Russian troops entered Berlin;
he had been incarcerated in the Gestapo's Berlin-Moabit
prison, where he wrote the eighty 'Moabit Sonnets' while
waiting to be executed for his opposition to the Nazi regime.
The quote is from the lines inscribed on the back wall of the
prison, which is preserved as a memorial in the Moabit district
of Berlin. I want to thank my old friend John Dickson for
introducing me to Haushofer's poems.

11

Regentropfen aus den Bäumen ('Raindrops from the trees')
I am indebted to the New Zealand musicologist Peter Russell's
book *Johannes Brahms and Klaus Groth: The Biography of a
Friendship* (Aldershot / Burlington, Ashgate Publishing, 2006)
for its wealth of information on the complex collaborative
friendship between the composer Johannes Brahms and the
poet Klaus Groth. I read Russell's book alongside the Groth
texts, in the Staatsbibliothek zu Berlin, where Dr Jochen Haug
was a great help, and became a good friend. Of the thirteen
poems by Groth that Brahms set to music, this is one of three
I've found recordings of – in this case as WoO post. 23 (also
known as 'Nachklang' Op. 59/4), with Jessye Norman, soprano,
and Daniel Barenboim, piano (*Brahms Lieder,* Hamburg:
Polydor International/Deutsche Grammophon, 1983).

15

*. . . man is an animal suspended in webs of significance he himself
has spun.*

Clifford Geertz, *The Interpretation of Cultures*, citing Max
Weber. The extended quote is:

> Believing, with Max Weber, that man is an animal
> suspended in webs of significance he himself has spun,
> I take culture to be those webs, and the analysis of it to
> be therefore not an experimental science in search of law
> but an interpretive one in search of meaning. (p.5)

16

Dies ist nun alles und ist nicht genug.
Bertolt Brecht, 'Motto', in Michael Hofmann (ed.), *Twentieth-
Century German Poetry* (New York: Farrar, Straus and Giroux,
2006).

17

Wo nur ein Blümchen blühte,
Das blühten gleich sie mit
Klaus Groth, *Hundert Blätter: Paralipomena zum Quickborn*,
the unsuccessful 1854 Hochdeutsch supplement to the hugely
popular Plattdüütsch poems of the original *Quickborn* (1852).

Wie traulich war das Fleckchen
Also from *Hundert Blätter*, one of a suite of three poems set to
music by Brahms as Himweh I, II, and III and published in
1874 (Op. 63/7-9). The other two are 'O wüsst ich doch den
Weg zurück' (II), and 'Ich sah als Knabe Blumen blühn' (III).

20

Die Leiden des jungen Werthers.
Johann Wolfgang von Goethe's epistolary novel *The Sorrows of
Young Werther* was first published in 1774. Its plot centres on
the impossibility of Werther's passionate love for Lotte (real
name Charlotte Buff in Goethe's own life) and his consequent

suicide – said to have been responsible for *Werther-Fieber*
(Werther-Fever), with resulting copycat suicides by young men
disappointed in love. My Werther-pigeon didn't kill himself,
but he came close by tempting the cat to do the job for him.

23

Der kleine Mann mit dem interessanten, ausdrucksvollen
Kopfe auf einem leider verwachsenen Körper war ein glühender
Sozialdemokrat; konnte aber erst später öffentlich als solcher
auftreten.
('The little man with the interesting, expressive head on an
unfortunately deformed body was an incandescent social
democrat; however, it was only later that he was first able to act
as such.')
Wilhelm Joseph Blos (1849–1927), in *Denkwürdigkeiten*
eines Sozialdemokraten (*Memorabilia of a Social Democrat*),
(München: G. Birk, 1914).

24

seine mit Geist und Humor gewürzte Konversation
Blos (1914)

25

seine oft sehr hübschen Verse konnten wegen des gelehrten
Ballastes, mit dem sie gepackt waren, nicht in die Masse dringen
Blos (1914)

26

The vanity of art
Milan Kundera, *The Unbearable Lightness of Being* (New York:
Harper and Row, 1984).

29

liebenswürdig und geistvoll ('amiable and witty')
Blos (1914)

An Theodora Wedde
Als Dank für Geschenk einer Traube
Johannes Wedde, *Gesammelte Werke*, Erster Band (Hamburg:
Verlag von Hermann Grüning, 1894), p.146a.

'Zum Gedächtnis' (1876)
Wedde, Zweiter Band (1894), p.17.

30

Walle, Regen, walle nieder,
Wecke meine alten Lieder,
Die wir in der Türe sangen,
Wie die Tropfen draussen klangen!
Groth, 1854; set to music and published by Brahms as
'Regenlied', Op. 59/3 (8 Lieder, 1870–73).

31

Schweiss und Blut
Wedde, 'Zum Gedächtnis', in *Gesammelte Werke* (1894).

'Day that Time Forgot'
Poly Styrene / Marianne Joan Elliott-Said, track 4 on
Translucence by Poly Styrene (Receiver, 11 May 1999). Lyric by
Poly Styrene.

32

immer nur meine Eintönigkeit,
mein Schattenzwang
Gottfried Benn, 'Gewisse Lebensabende', in Hofmann (2006).

33

. . . politisch ohne Vorurteil
Correspondence of Friedrich Engels – Quelle: Briefe April
1883 bis Dezember 1887; #657, #335 – Engels an Pasquale
Martignetti / in Benevento – London, 21. Mai 1887. Das
Elektronische Archiv (DEA).

34

*The sadness was form, the happiness content. Happiness filled the
space of sadness.*
Kundera (1984).

35

'Look at life with the eyes of a child'
Käthe Kollwitz, quoted in exhibition signage, Käthe Kollwitz
Museum, Fasanenstraße, Berlin.

36

Würde Welt plötzlich anders,
wir weinten
Ernst Meister, 'Monolog der Menschen', in Hofmann (2006).

37

Mit Heimweh und Brechreiz beladene Schiffe
Günter Grass, 'Klappstühle', in Hofmann (2006).

38

We are not desperate idiots of history
Rudi Dutschke, interview with Günter Gaus, in 'Rudi
Dutschke zu Protocol', *Voltaire Flugschrift* No.17 (1967).
English translation cited in Pasquali and Kalnins, Universität
Bremen / Jacobs University Bremen, 2009. The expanded
statement by Dutschke reads: 'We can change. We are not

desperate idiots of history, unable to take their destiny in their own hands.'

45

Nature herself is sublimely eloquent
Alexander von Humboldt, *Personal Narrative of Travels of the Equinoctial Regions of the New Continent during Years 1799–1804* (London, 1814), vol. 1, pp.34–35.

51

I didn't know I loved so many things and I had to wait until sixty to find it out sitting by the window on the Prague–Berlin train watching the world disappear as if on a journey of no return
Nâzim Hikmet Ran, 19 April 1962. Trans. Randy Blasing and Mutlu Konuk (1993).

52

Tahir, Taksim, Tempelhof:
Das Feld gehört uns allen!
Poster printed by *Die Linke* ('Mach mit!' die-linke-neukoelln.de), Kreuzberg, Berlin, 2013.

53

der Narziβmus der kleinen Differenzen
. . . the narcissism of small differences . . .
Freud, *Civilization and Its Discontents* (1930).

58

Er ist eigentlich dumm aber auch irgendwie nicht
Hannah Arendt, letter to Karl Jaspers, Jerusalem 1961.
Cited in Amos Elon's introduction to Arendt's *Eichmann in Jerusalem: A Report on the Banality of Evil* (Penguin Classics, Kindle Edition).

59

'The banality of evil'

The phrase for which Arendt was castigated after *Eichmann in Jerusalem* was published in 1963. It appears as the subheading of Arendt's title and as the final phrase of its final chapter.

60

<u>p</u>   *á*   <u>*ci*</u>
venez   *sans*

'Wit: Voltaire and Frederick the Great', Hannibal and Me, 23 Nov 2008. andreaskluth.org/2008/11/23/wit-voltaire-and-frederick-the-great

61

Solch ein Gewimmel möcht ich sehn,
Auf freiem Grund mit Freien Volke stehn.

Goethe, *Faust* – masonry inscription on the façade of the GDR-era Haus des Kindes, 19 Strausberger Platz, Karl Marx Allee, Berlin. Described as the first 'Kinderkaufhaus' in the whole of Germany, it was opened on 18 October 1954.

62

Life goes on

The Chills, 'Doledrums' (1984). Lyrics by Martin Phillipps.

63

I'm so scared

The Chills, 'Pink Frost' (1984). Lyrics by Martin Phillipps.

64

Es ist Zeit, daß es Zeit wird.
Paul Celan, 'Corona', in Hofmann (2006).

65

Wenn die Ideen begraben sind
Kommen die Knochen heraus
Volker Braun, 'Nach dem Massaker der Illusionen', *Tumulus*
(Suhrkamp Verlag, 1998).

66

. . . *eine stunde lang war eine*
stunde da wo weder du noch ich vorher gewesen war.
Norbert Hummelt, 'pans stunde', in *Pans Stunde – Gedichte*
(München: Luchterhand Literaturverlag/Verlagsgruppe,
Random House, 2011).

67

In jedem Werk gibt es die Stelle, an der es uns kühl anweht
wie die kommende Frühe.
Volker Braun, 'Benjamin in den Pyrenäen', *Lustgarten*
(Suhrkamp Verlag, Preußen, 1996).

72

. . . *im Herbstmanöver der Zeit*
Ingeborg Bachmann, 'Herbstmanöver', in Hofmann (2006).

73

Wake up (wake up)
Grab a brush and put a little make-up . . .
System of a Down, 'Chop Suey!', track #5 on *Toxicity*, written
by Daron Malakian and Serj Tankian. American Recordings,
2001. Pianist Viktoriya Yermolyeva's and drummer Gabor's
version was instrumental but many in the SO36 audience in
Kreuzberg, Berlin, sang along, 21 August 2014.

76

'a two-volume edition of the essays
and shorter writings of Leibniz
modern American translations'.

Quoted from a letter from my second cousin Peter Nicholas
Wedde, Monday 27 October 2014, in which he describes
affectionately an exchange of letters with my great-uncle
(Peter's uncle) Fritz in Mexico, about 1958, when Peter was a
student in Dunedin and when Fritz had recently resurfaced.
Peter adds that 'Fritz must have gone to some trouble to buy
and post [the Leibniz books], which doesn't quite fit with his
apparent reluctance to spend money, or go to too much trouble
with his business affairs'.

Acknowledgements

In the mid-1950s our family left New Zealand for what was then East Pakistan, where my father had a job at the remote Kharnaphuli paper mill. The company hired teachers for foreign staff, and it was the second of these, (retired) Herr Professor Robert Lübker, who first taught me German. In 1995 while working in Germany I met up with dear Professor Lübker in a restaurant in Hamburg – he was ninety-something years old but ate a good lunch with a couple of glasses of Riesling and talked energetically around mouthfuls of fresh asparagus. At the end of our lunch, I thanked him for his long-ago introductions to German language and some German poetry. I thank him again now with all my heart and remember him with gratitude and love.

After East Pakistan, my brother Dave and I were sent to school in England while our parents went elsewhere for work. We boarded at school in Somerset in the early 1960s. The headmaster R.C. Davy taught German and I'm grateful for his scrupulous lessons, which I remembered long past my time in his classes and into subsequent mediocre classes elsewhere.

In Berlin in 2013–14, while benefitting from the generous Creative New Zealand Berlin Writers' Residency, I was grateful for the friendship and hospitality of neighbours Klaus, Petra, Melanie and Jessie, who owned the Blattwerk Blumenhandlung flower shop near my residency apartment on Niederbarnimstraße. *Viel Glück und Freude!*

Tania Wehrs was the Berlin apartment manager, whose thoughtful advice to me included where to get a good secondhand bike. I thank her for this and a great many more hospitable kindnesses.

The *Staatsbibliothek zu Berlin* website promises that its *Fachreferent* or specialist consultant Dr Jochen Haug – *hilft Ihnen gerne weiter* – will be glad to assist you further. This was true in the case of my many importunate requests, in spite of which we became friends. I thank Jochen for his help and his friendship.

I was fortunate to meet the poet Norbert Hummelt, among other writers, in Berlin; I thank him and them for their openness and generous hospitality.

My German relative Detlef Reepen is a journalist and TV and radio presenter. There's an image of him holding a snake called Zakura up to a microphone on the kinder.wdr.de website. Zakura has lived at Detlef's home for some years. The expertise and friendship I have continued to enjoy involve our mutual human ancestors on the Reepen side of the family, and I thank Detlef for his warmth and generosity and for sharing ancestral Reepen knowledge.

Another cousin, Peter Nicholas Wedde, is the New Zealand branch of the family's senior Wedde historian. It was Peter who filled in some detail about my great-uncle Fritz, the family's mystery man, who disappeared about 1905, and reappeared in the mid-1950s near Torreón, Mexico, where it seemed he had built an observatory and written a paper, 'A New Hypothesis or Theory of the Universe'. Fritz and Peter exchanged letters about 1958, and Fritz sent Peter 'a two-volume edition of the essays and shorter writings of Leibniz, modern American translations'. I thank Peter for some marvellous conversations, and other family members for theirs.

I acknowledge and thank the New Zealand musicologist, Germanist and singer Peter Russell for his fascinating book, *Johannes Brahms and Klaus Groth: The Biography of a Friendship*, in which I was able to read about the relationship between the composer and my obscurely related Platdüütsch poet.

A special thanks to my dear friend the poet John Dickson who died on 4 February 2017. It was John who introduced me to the work of Albrecht Georg Haushofer and his 'Moabit Sonnets'. I visited the prison, preserved as a memorial in Moabit, Berlin, where Haushofer was held prior to his execution by the Nazis.

I am profoundly grateful to Fergus Barrowman, my publisher at Victoria University Press, for his continued support; and to Ashleigh Young for her adroit and sympathetic editing of this hoarder's text.

Ian Wedde was born in Blenheim, New Zealand, in 1946. He lives in Auckland with his wife, the screenwriter Donna Malane. His first small book was *Homage to Matisse* (London: Amphedesma Press, 1971). *The Little Ache – a German notebook* is his seventeenth.